Love's Prism
Reflections From
the Heart of a Woman

Alla Renée Bozarth

Sheed & Ward

Illustrations by Valerie Willson
Copyright © 1987
Alla Renée Bozarth

Sheed & Ward TM is a service of National Catholic Reporter Publishing, Inc.

Library of Congress Catalog Card Number: 86-63272

ISBN: 1-55612-044-3

Published by:

Sheed & Ward
115 E. Armour Blvd. P.O. Box 414292
Kansas City, MO 64141-4292

To order, call: (800) 821-7926

We have belonged to light,
and slowed to these particular bodies,
and shall return to light again.
And when we do, shall we remember then
that we have been these bodies, embracing
in sunlight in pure joy, and
that we have loved each other?

from *Sunday Memory*

Some of the poems in this book appear elsewhere:

"I have been asleep for ten years of my life" was first published as "Gynergy" in the poetry collection, *Gynergy,* Wisdom House Press, 1978.

"Travail" also first appeared in *Gynergy.*

"Love Mantra for Letting Go" was published in *Life is Goodbye/Life is Hello: Grieving Well through All Kinds of Loss,* CompCare Publications, 1982 and 1986; and in *Sparrow Songs,* Wisdom House Press, 1982. All copyrights are held by Alla Bozarth-Campbell (Alla Renée Bozarth).

Other poems in *Love's Prism* are from the unpublished manuscript entitled *Loving in the Open,* by Alla Renée Bozarth.

To my teachers—those who live
the questions well.

Contents

CHAPTER 1
LOVING MYSELF

Dear Stranger, Dear Self,

So hard to love. You the strangest, you the most elusive. How can I love you when I do not even know you, dare not even name you? How can I begin to love you when I do not even know what love is?

You are—**I am.** You are the one in me who speaks forth being, who moves and is alive. You are the free and bound one, the one who hides and calls herself by name in secret. Who are you?

Anna Karenina told herself on her last ride toward death that she didn't know herself any more than the strangers who nodded at her, pretending to know her. "All I know are my appetites." But she was the heart's child of a man, after all. Not a real woman, but Tolstoy's imaginative manikin.

I am a real woman. Surely I know myself by more than my appetites.

Surely.

1

I am concerned with the question of love. A question that begins with this most awkward, unknown person—myself. It begins here because how else can I discover the way to unlock the door inside me that opens toward loving others?

Love your neighbor as yourself. Not more, not less. How can such a miracle be achieved—to love my neighbor as myself, and not to love him more, or her less?

So I begin here, with this most difficult and most basic of loves, the love of myself. How can I find you, my Self, in order to speak to you?

I have to go all the way down, all the way back, all the way in to my own beginnings. Who loved me first, in the beginning? What was the first love I knew? Who *was* my first love?

In the beginning, Mother. I was held close in the stretching nest of my mother's womb.

In those moments when my mother failed to love me before I was born (yes, I know those moments burned in her), in the moments when her longing for me left her, her body loved me because it held me—and hated me because it was bound to me. Her body gave me time, gave me life, and even in resisting me, her body was first to love me.

I go back to that time and realize that never since then have I been held enough. To be held all day and all night, to be cherished with no letting go before the human urgency of the later lust for freedom, to be caressed with such constancy as was in my mother's blood! But the memory is unreal, a bitter self-deceiving illusion, for I was not my Self then. I was not even human. Not even a memory, only a wistful grown-up's myth.

The time I slept serene in my mother's inner nest, I never knew anything of love. It was the time before awakening, The time before I could hear the word *love*, or know it by its absence. In the time before the beginning, there was only fusion. Before birth there is blissful confusion. This is not love, for love requires separateness, and longing. It requires a lover and a beloved. Before birth there is pure unity, and no need for reunion. No lover and loved, but the seed of love to come. No real being, and no real possibility. Only with the heartbreaking separation of birth does longing awaken, and only with longing can love be.

In the separation from my mother's holding body, I became a separate possibility. A being floating free in time. Or the promise of being, held in the possibility of time. In the first despair of being born, human life takes form because *longing* has come.

Then appetite arose in me. The first groping for my mother's breast, the strangeness of finding food outside her body, of struggling—already beginning to create myself in struggle—against chill and noise and all the elemental harshness of the outside world. Floating in the waters of my mother's body between time and no-time, there was no Self because there was only self—She and I as One. Now Self became a reality because none of this glare, none of this alien fragmentation could in any way be part of me. My mother betrayed me by withdrawing from around me! Not that I left the nest of her body willingly, but that she squeezed herself away from me—as a woman I know it was more her labor than mine. She delivered herself free in the moment of my birth!

With my mother's release I had been borne into the necessity of fighting for my own survival. Now my mother had to prove her love. I had to seek and she had to provide and prove. And neither of us would forget that she would never again be able to hold me enough, to hold me as before. And though the way she fed me was a new delight (and *delight* itself was new), it lacked the perfection we had known before when she and I were one.

The birth of longing is the beginning of the quest for love. I am uneasy in facing the reality that longing itself is born from a primary sense of betrayal. Love is suddenly known by need, and by absence, and by a hunger that the breast only begins to satisfy. Perhaps the question of love really is a question of one's most basic appetite after all.

From the moment of longing's appearance in the betrayal of birth, for each of us life becomes a game of hiding from one's deepest, secret craving for love, the insatiability of the craving, the skepticism behind it; and despite this, despite the fear and shame surrounding the need, there is also the game of seeking, and groping with some degree of trust.

How can the longing for love ever be fulfilled? The hurt child in each of us knowing love only as *care*—being cared for, and learning to respond by caring in return. That simple. Saints through the ages have answered simply: love is gained by loving others. By creating love where love does not exist. But can love be created, or is it simply given? And can one love others without first loving oneself? And can one love oneself without first being loved by another?

Dear Self, your own dark game of self-torture circles frantically around your own consistent failure to love and to be loved enough. How to break the circle and call off the game?

First, know that you don't have to overcome the lack of love all by yourself, or all at once. Love *is* a gift. You can't make it appear by magic. It is a grace. It comes, in its own time and way. Whether you are the lover or the beloved, you can only receive love as a gift.

I believe in love as I believe in the Holy Spirit—that love is a reality and an energy in the universe so powerful that it takes form and becomes a living presence, a more-than-human, cosmic personal presence that is felt and known, recognized intuitively and immediately by those prepared for it.

Though you cannot create love yourself since love creates itself and comes as it wills, you can prepare yourself for it. Love comes to those who are prepared. They draw love to themselves, they attract it. You, then, if you seek love, must make yourself attractive to love. When you are ready, you will become so attractive to love that love will come.

You can prepare yourself for love the way a Rainmaker prepares for the coming of rain.

The Rainmaker does not threaten the heavens, does not weep to mock the clouds, does not cajole or insist, pine or pout. The Rainmaker simply aligns her spirit with the holy spirit of the rain. Making her home in the dry place, she waits and gently calls upon the rain by the natural attraction of letting be.

In the arid places of the southwest or the deserts of the far west, the Rainmaker is often heard singing for rain while going about her ordinary tasks. She tends her weaving, dyes her cloth, cooks and cleans, all the time making herself one with the longed-for rain. In time, the rain comes, and comes to the Rainmaker's place before any other. Where others danced noisily or petitioned loudly in near despair, she only sang quietly to herself, went about life in a harmonious manner, and waited. The spirit of the rain that had resisted all others could not resist her.

Love is like the rain. It comes when we become still, when we make peace with ourselves and our surroundings as equal parts of nature. Listening to the inner rhythms of things and joining with them, turning oneself toward the grace within nature, providing a space for a new presence— this is what allows love like rain to show itself, what attracts and invites it to come and be in our midst.

If there is a weeping, lonely infant inside you, my Self, there is also the Rainmaker. Let her take the longing infant in her arms and soothe her with the rhythms of her faith, the wholeness of her grace.

The very moment that one begins to prepare for love, love comes. Preparation for love can only be by means of love. The moment when the Rainmaker sets up her tent in the arid place, clouds begin to gather invisibly. From then on so long as the will toward love remains, the manifesting of love has been set in motion. The moment of its self-revelation is its moment of full ripening and presence.

Others have written about love's many forms and faces. I want to tell you about love's light and dark faces, its silver and gold forms. They are called *Agape* and *Eros*.

Both Agape and Eros have desire: Agape desires the well-being of the beloved; Eros desires union with the beloved.

Agape is not only desire, but a well-wishing attitude. Sometimes Agape has been called impersonal, or love-in-general. I don't believe that love can be impersonal or in general. Agape is personal and specific; it flows within and among persons as a well-wishing attitude toward the wholeness of things. Its specific is the whole, but this is not the same as the vague abstractness of the "general." Agape loves being. Loves being itself, the being of things in themselves. Agape's virtue is integrity. In loving being it says, "What is, is." Agape is realistic.

Eros is chiefly desire. It longs to bring things into communion, into union, to join and weave and make relationships. Eros's virtue is creativity. Eros loves into being. Longs things into being. Is longing itself—the power to draw beings together. Eros values becoming. In creating by loving things into being, Eros asks, "What new thing can come from this?" Eros longs to make the ideal real.

The Rainmaker waits and yearns—and Agape and Eros are present, Agape blessing her waiting and Eros blessing her yearning. By letting be and longing for what is to come she places herself in their presence. In the presence of Agape she observes the reality of death-dealing dryness, and she wishes the earth well. Eros enables her to see the possibility of life-giving rain, to see deeply and live into her vision. Eros teaches the Rainmaker how to make a space for rain to come and show itself, how to to create unity between earth and sky, a place of meeting and bringing forth of new life. Waiting and singing, she serves, she prepares.

The Rainmaker is not passive in her waiting. She moves with the movement of life around her. There is a sandpainting on the kitchen wall made by a Navaho woman, Pearl Watchman. On the back it says, "Made while singing for rain." The sandpainting was made with sand and water, created by Eros and Pearl out of the very thing longed for. In the act of sandpainting, the longing and the gift become one.

Love is called upon by means of love already given and present. It is the raw material of longing and creating; it is born out of itself. <u>What is desired is now and not-yet.</u> In the beginning of longing, love is present like the seeds of rain, not the full-bodied, thunder-driven gift of water. Fullness will come in time. It's been promised. You have only to put yourself in harmony with its spirit, and love like rain will come, even to the most arid places of your being, the driest places of your deserted soul.

Love is useful. Love is realistic. It is longing and alive. Integrity and creativity. Agape and Eros. Waiting and yearning. Working and singing. Be patient, my Self, and have faith while you sing for the gift.

Like the Rainmaker, you must first understand that you are a creature upon the earth. You have been given to the earth and its inhabitants, and they have been given to you. You are a creature who can create. You yourself were loved into being by God, who formed you in Her heart before you were born. Within your form She breathed the power of creation; you too have the gift of calling forth something new into the universe. You are part animal, part angel. To you the power and the possibility have been given—to call down the bodies of the stars, your fellow creatures, and to make new shapes with their light for the joy and use of yourself and others. The special grace of your nature is that you are both a beloved creature and a loving creator.

The Rainmaker is also an artist. She makes paintings for kitchen walls as well as for rain. The gifts of her art are sand and water and the spirit within her and them; these gifts already contain the rain, in the same moment that they call it to come forth. The yearning and the fulfilling are one, as Eros and Agape are one in love's self-giving revelation.

With the raw material of love's longing you can create, like the Rainmaker who creates with the seeds of rain. You can create realities, relationships, works of art, ideas, children. You can create your Self. <u>But should you fail to use the gift, it will withdraw from you.</u>

It is an abiding gift only so long as you use it. If water is not made into something beyond itself, it dries up and disappears. Love can also disappear, as quickly as it appeared. It will not tolerate being wasted. Neglecting the gift is the same as rejecting it. Love must serve usefully in order to reign, and where it cannot reign, it cannot dwell for long.

Honor the faces of love within you. When you enter the presence of Agape and Eros, know that you are in a sacred presence. Worship them. Worship them by recognizing their worth and using it wisely. These faces can appear as different from one another as the faces of the Holy Spirit, which artists have expressed in the forms of the dove and the flame. The dove is light, serene, and gentle, while the tongue of fire destroys and burns as it purifies and gives new form, turning lead into gold. But the dove and the fire are one. Like lights in a prism, they show forth many colors all at once, create many images and pictures, aspects of the same substance, often in seeming contradiction.

Light is like the disparate aspects of love and the Holy Spirit. We know from science that light can be observed as flowing waves, or it can be observed as particles, or quanta. It can be observed as one or the other, but not as both at the same time. This is because of the limitations of our observation and understanding, not because of any limitation in the nature of light. Even scientists have to speak in poetry to describe the unreasonable mysteries of physical reality, One young scientist has called the problem of observing and describing light the "Quantum Koan," or the "Riddle of the Wavicle." Love also has contradictions which are true. It doesn't seem possible or logical that love means simultaneously letting be, as Agape, and longing for something new, as Eros—but that is precisely the nature of love. A contradiction, as the nature of light. As the gentleness of the dove and the ferocity of fire in the same Holy Spirit. Perhaps the contradictions are not in light, or love, or the Holy Spirit, but only in ourselves. In our too-small, too-concentrated ability to see, and to speak.

In observing the properties of light as waves, you are struck with the unconscious understanding that light is equally revealed as particles. When reflecting on the Holy Spirit as the graceful dove, you are unconsciously disconcerted by the memory of the same Spirit as a consuming flame. When love comes and is felt in your midst, you are also aware of the lingering emptiness where love is not felt at all. And when love is absent, you can only know this by having first known its presence.

How can you honor all the faces of love, its presence and its absence, in your life? You know the words. Patience. Forgiveness. Honesty. Esteem. Acceptance. You may have learned a little how to express these things toward others, but how can you bear them toward your Self? Here is the contradiction that is too much for the mind. Only by bearing them toward your Self can you really bear them toward others; and only by bearing them toward others and receiving them from others can you know how to bear them toward your Self. This two-sided truth is the "wavicle" of love.

Receive and use the gift of Agape toward yourself. Let yourself be. This is to accept that you will fail in love, again and again. Receive the gift of Eros and know that striving is necessary to life, that despite the failure to love or to be loved, you must and will continue to seek love, and love will continue to come.

Your own inadequacy is so much at the heart of your need for love. More than anything, you need enough love to accept that you will fail yourself and others as others will fail you. When you can face this, you will be able to accept the inadequacy of others and not blame them for failing you because of the frailty you share.

There is also the need to accept the good that you are. You were created because someone longed you into being. You were created in the image of a longing, good, and creative God. You are worthy of receiving and giving love. In order to live you must love and be loved. Love this necessity in yourself.

You are a woman. All your life you have placed yourself last. With your mother's milk came the message that all others—especially men and children—must come before you in life. And these others were also taught that you should come last! Don't expect them suddenly to put you first now. You must learn to do this for yourself, to give others the joy of giving to you as you have known the joy of giving to them. And to teach yourself the joy of receiving. It is blessed to give, yes, but it is also blessed to receive. For givers, the greatest gift is being received. Learning to receive yourself graciously is something you must work on. Learning to love yourself without shame, without excuse, without withholding—self-love without guilt. That's the miracle of the century! What woman has ever achieved it? We've got to keep trying—*you've* got to keep working on it. Love yourself, dear Self, as a woman worthy, created in God's image, and worthy of being loved. Simply by being who you are, you are worthy.

All your female life you've been given society's message that you are unworthy and unacceptable for being female. You were made to feel unworthy for what you *are*, so you tried from tiny girlhood to make up for the unnamed lack in you, to become worthy for what you *do*. You became a servant, a giver, a lover of others, to prove yourself and be approved of. If you did well or looked good enough, your good works or your good looks could make you acceptable and lovable. If not, misery and failure were your lot.

In ancient times, sterility in a woman was considered proof of her failure to compensate for the sin of being born female. In modern times, sterility of the soul is often self-imposed by our willingness to wallow in self-hate.

Being rejected by others, how can you accept yourself? How can you have self-esteem if others despise you not only for what you do or don't do, but for what you are—or aren't?

If only one person somewhere on this earth can love you for who you are, for the particular miracle that you are, a woman like no other, a human being created uniquely in God's glory—and if you can truly accept this love—then you will know that it's enough simply to be. Receive the well-wishing of Agape and you can begin to be healed of the wounds where others have rejected you, denied you Eros, and sinned against you. Not only must you love yourself in order to love others, but you must receive love from yourself in order to receive it from others. Whether the gift comes from yourself, from God, or from another person, to be able to receive it is the beginning of your own healing.

You are worthy of love for who you are. You don't have to do anything beyond being yourself in order to be loved. Use the gift of love within you. Use Eros for your own healing and renewal. Meet yourself anew. Find the gifts and needs within you and bring them into relationship within you. Create new unities within you. Join the parts of yourself. Learn to treat yourself with infinite kindness and tenderness. There is no shame in kindness. Become for yourself the kindest of mothers, the tenderest of lovers.

This is how to become born again—to become your own mother and give birth to yourself all over again, gently, lovingly, knowingly; and then to nurture and cherish the new being within you to new maturity. Take the dejected baby within you into your mothering arms and love her, love yourself. You can do this because God is within you to teach you, and because you know women and men in your own life who have given you acceptance, esteem, forgiveness, honesty, and patience, and have shown you what love is and how love feels.

Remember what you learned of love from your own real mother. She was your first teacher. She gave you your vocation to love. By her example she showed you how to love others. Because she knew her own needs and gifts she used them to help others. Because she knew what it was to be homeless as a young child after the Russian Revolution, she made it her work as a Russian American to find new homes for displaced persons from around the world. She showed you how in your work as a therapist you can help persons who feel displaced to find their way home within themselves. Your mother taught you well by her example how to love others—but she did not teach you to love yourself, because no one had ever taught her that special kind of love. You must look to her love for you, rather than her example in loving herself, in order to discover how to love yourself. And when she hovered over you too much in the beginning, that was not always love, but often fear, unsure concern, her own self-doubt and inadequacy that drove her, her despair in ever loving you enough, or well. And later when she withdrew from you, that too was fear—fear of losing you, of her own uncontrollable longing to bind you too close to her, her fear of your rejection. Learn from those times what fear can do to make love fail. But learn from the good times in-between when she loved you well how love is a power that can heal and make things grow.

Then, difficult as loving yourself is, you will discover that it is possible and necessary, and that the necessity and possibility for love are within you. To discover this is to receive the holiest gift, to become transformed, fulfilling the promise made in the Scriptures that we shall become as gods and goddesses. Then you will be able to say your own name to yourself, the joined names of both your parents, the Russian and the French: *Alla Renée*. It means the Goddess Reborn.

Alleluia.

CHAPTER 2
LOVING WOMEN

Dear Mother, Dear Sister,

How long it's taken me to find you! How I have longed for you without knowing it all my life! And now, having let go of the grief I felt in our separation, I celebrate at last being able to embrace you in the sun, my mother, my daughter, my sister, my friend.

So much has separated us for too many thousands of years. We are so close, you and I, sharing the awesome gift and burden of a female body, sharing common female experience, and yet only now do we begin timidly to look in one another's eyes with recognition.

We are like the women in the First Garden—Lilith and Eve, the first gardeners and growers of living things from the body of the earth. Men have told their story through fear-bent eyes these many years. Here is a woman's version of the ancient myth: Lilith and Adam were created from the earth's body in the image of the Creator. Together they cultivated the earth and named their fellow creatures. Since it was given to Lilith's body to bring forth new beings of their kind, Adam soon became jealous of his partner's life-bearing powers, her special creative link with their Maker. As God had formed them from the dust and given birth to them, the woman also was able to breathe new life from her own body into her daughters and sons. Adam was unaware of his own subtle participation in this process, and he was too impatient to discover his own nurturing powers. He resented God for favoring the woman with the visible power to give life, and he grew bitter toward her. Soon he became violent in his hostility and forced Lilith to flee the garden and their life together, and like many of the animals, she was left to raise her children alone. But Adam soon became lonely. He began to realize his error. He longed for Lilith to return, but she feared for her children and stayed at a safe distance. God had compassion for Adam. One day while he was sleeping, God formed Eve, being well pleased with the first woman, and sent this second woman to tend the garden which Adam had neglected in his grief, and to restore order to the earth. Adam rejoiced in his new companion, and for a time he was contrite for his cruel banishment of Lilith and truly responsive and kind to Eve. But Eve also swelled with the magic of life and bore children, and Adam forgot his first lesson and also grew jealous of her. This was unfortunate, since she could not help it if the Creator had bestowed the powers of life upon her. It was part of the gift of her nature, as it was part of Adam's nature to give life more subtly. Eve refused to be frightened away by Adam. She stood firm, and insisted that he be a responsible parent to their children. He began to realize that he, too, could nurture them and care for them in his own way. He also was necessary. One day, while Adam was watching the children and Eve was working in the garden, Eve became aware of how lonely she was. She began to weep, wishing that someone like her would come. Adam was a good companion, but there were limitations to their relationship. Perhaps he felt them too. God saw Eve crying, and God also saw Lilith crying in her own garden beyond the stone wall which was between them. God arranged for the two women to hear one another weeping. Little did they know they were weeping for each other! Both women approached the wall which separated them, which kept Eve in and Lilith out. They began to dig at the wall, each from her own side.

Suddenly they saw each other through an opening they had made together. "You are like me!" they exclaimed together. And they embraced and dried each other's tears. Lilith took Eve into her garden, and then Eve invited Lilith to hers, and they exchanged knowledge each had learned in tilling the earth. Together, they founded agriculture and art, for both women also loved to weave with grasses and paint with vegetable dyes. Adam saw how good their friendship was, and now he too realized that he also longed for a companion like himself. The Creator gave birth to a new son, and he joined the three grown-up human beings and became Adam's brother as Eve had become Lilith's longed-for sister. They realized the necessity for friendship was as strong as the necessity for food and children, and they taught their children to value friendship as they valued life itself.

You and I have also had a wall built up between us. We also have wept for each other, not even knowing that it was the abiding friendship of another woman that we wanted. But God arranged for us to hear each other, and gave us the strength and courage to seek each other. We dug away at our own walls, and the reward of our labors is this precious gift of true friendship, a gift we can share with others, with other women, and with those men who are truly our brothers.

Because the old walls existed inside us for so long, we haven't been able to tear them down all at once. Bit by bit we work at them, understanding what they are made of and how they were made. Bit by bit we free ourselves and celebrate each other.

What are these walls, these ancient grey walls inside us that divide us, my Sister?

The walls belong to a labyrinthine prison and are of double thickness. They have an internal and an external side—a membrane which forms from within ourselves, and a carapace formed by society. The walls wind within and around us, and though we cannot see over them, we can sometimes hear each other through them, and so come to discover thin places where we put our hands to the work of love in unmaking the barrier.

I believe that the components of the inner walls are chiefly these: fear, rivalry, and guilt.

The separating membrane inside you and me may appear quite smooth and even pliable. But this is deceptive. The inner wall is the toughest and most impervious. The inner wall contains and isolates us in the small prison of ourselves. Our frightened, rivalrous, and guilty selves.

Look inside with me, look into the inner labyrinth of your cellular being as I look into mine. We dare do this because now we are no longer alone. We have each other, and in many ways we are the same. Surely the same in what separates us. Once we face this fully, we'll be free to discover the inner and outer realities that unite and heal us. Now, my Sister, my Friend, together let us find what has divided—and so hurt and deprived—us.

I see myself a cell inside an opaque prison of fear. I locate this in my body somewhere near my solar plexus, in my bowels, and encaging my throat. It is a long, narrow membrane that begins in my bowels and is cut off at the choking closure of my throat, just before the organ of utterance. The membrane is a watery blue color, like a giant seablue teardrop that fills the cavity of my body and encloses it to keep me empty. Here I am both prisoner and prison. I see you so dimly, as one senses more than sees through sheets of falling water on a sunless day as twilight approaches, when heavy rain is no longer transparent but seems solid in its relentlessness. I do not recognize you.

My fear seems relentless and solid. I know it has thinness and is not substantial, but this doesn't matter. I am as locked within it as within hard cement.

What is my fear of you, Woman? Is it nothing more than my fear of my Self? The sudden undoing of all my sophisticated pretenses of *not* being afraid, *not* being guilty, *not* having endless depths of yearning? Is my fear of you the more subtle fear of facing my own true beauty in you, my own rightful pride in being Woman? What will it cost me to give up the carefully learned lie of false vanity and false modesty—my masks of female survival in a male world? What will it cost me to recognize my own inadequacy in you, and to see my own undeniable capability in your being? Are you, like me, free and not-free?

I am afraid of exposing myself to you because I will not be able to deceive you. You are too like me to be deceived. I would be more vulnerable in your presence than in any other. I would have to be more truthful, more simply honest with you than I can be even with myself. To face you, I would have to face myself. One thing in me dissolves this layer of the wall, and that is that I am of the age when one realizes that the only alternative to being vulnerable is being dead.

I am afraid that you will fail me, that you will turn away from me, that you will tell me what all mothers tell their daughters: "You can take care of yourself." I am afraid that you will neither nurture me nor receive nurture from me. As women, we do not nurture each other well or know how to receive nurture well, because our mothers have taught us to be mothers from the moment of our birth. This comes from a culture which worships a male god and worships males as gods. The Madonna and Child is always a Woman and her Son, never a Woman and her Daughter. The divine myth is the myth of mother and son, which, in patriarchal religion, achieves both salvation of the female through motherhood, and divinization of the male through her total worship. Even now among friends of our own generation, there are women who will nurture their male children into their forties and fifties, but who deprive their female children of like nurturing from early infancy onward. We are taught to give, not to receive—and we are taught to give to males, not to each other.

I am also afraid that you will take too much from me, that because we have been deprived, one or both of us will be too hungry and will take too much from the other. We do not know how to give to each other without giving ourselves away.

I am afraid that if I accept your care and your nurturing, I will have to surrender my strength to you. You will become my mother and I will become a child, and lose the integrity of my own strong adult womanhood. I do not want to be a weak and leeching child. I do not want you to be the all-powerful Great Mother. I want, instead, to be free to support and be supported by you, with both of us always mindful of the intrinsic dignity, power, and freedom of the other. I yearn to receive the gifts of your care, but the essential gift must be respect for my adult reality. I yearn to show you my deep care for you, but I do not want to take any part of yourself away from you. We must meet each other as equals who can alternately give and receive support, healing, care, love.

I begin to see you more clearly through the thinning wall of my fear. It no longer chokes me. My gift of speech comes back to me. I may call out to you yet, from within the melting bubble of my fear.

I am prisoner inside another membrane. This one is made of greygreen sand. It exists up and down the length of my arms and legs, feet and hands. It is a scratchy, gritty, glass-like layer of divisive rivalry.

You were my rival in tricking our mother into treating us like sons, and in attracting our father's tender admiration. You were my rival in intelligence at school. My rival in beauty before men's eyes. My rival in keeping the devotion of my children. Even now you may be my rival in work, in self-liberation, in feminist consciousness or selfless devotion! There is no end to the ways we can invent to paint *Woman Keep Out* over our hearts. It is all so foolish, so unnecessary, so silly and so tragic.

I am willing to peel this abrasive layer off my bones and free myself to reach, stretch, dance, work, run, embrace. I want to let go of the sandpaper in my soul that keeps you at arm's length.

One wall remains. The last, innermost, thickest membrane. I do not want to see it. To confront it I have to be chased all through the inner maze, as if some terrifying judge forces me deeper, deeper into the labyrinth of my prison. I feel trapped, as if I am being forced to the place of my own execution at the very center of the complex structure. I throw myself against the dirty yellow walls of these more hidden tunnels and passageways to slow the inevitable coming to the core of the place. Finally I'm here. There is no escaping my guilt. I try to hide it in the central cell of my being. It is muddy yellow in color, and I have trouble locating it in my body. Perhaps it's in the liver or gall bladder! But it's there in some central encasing organ of myself, and it colors my blood, my tears, and seeps into my skin whether I permit it or not.

Why am I guilty toward you, my Sister?

Because I have deprived you as much as myself by closing myself from you. Because I have taken from you and given to you erratically and incompletely. Because I have left you over and over to give my loving care to men and to children. Because I have used you to criticize myself. Because I have rejected myself in you, and I have rejected you in myself. Because I have been ungenerous with you, as with myself. Because I have withheld praise from you when it was deeply deserved. Because I have not told you my true feelings for you. Because I have not wept in your arms or held you in mine as you wept. Because I have not laughed enough with you. Because we have not played together. Because we have doubted ourselves and failed to teach each other. Because I put you last, even after myself sometimes, because sometimes you are more myself than I am, and I do not want this to be generally known. Because I have loved myself so little, and so have loved you even less. Forgive me, forgive me, my Sister, my Mother, my Daughter, my Friend. I cannot bear the burden of having loved you unwell.

There are no more walls within me . . . that I can see.

Will you look outward with me, now, to see what separates us in the world? We are divided and conquered by outer walls of social institutions.

The outer shell of our prison walls is harder, but it is not as tough as the inner membranes. The membranes expand stubbornly and dissolve slowly. These outer walls wrongly concern us more because they are thicker and harder, but they are not as dangerous to us as those hidden inner layers. These outer walls are brittle and are easier to break down directly. I see them composed chiefly of our insecurity with men, children, and work. I do not say that men, children, and work always come between us, but that often our inability to say No to men, children, and work comes between us. All of these certainly can claim more of ourselves than we can healthily give, but givers that we are by training, we try. Often we pull it off; often we fail. When we fail, we fail everyone. Better to change our own standards than to be continually set up to overachieve or go to pieces.

How easy it is for us seldom to see another adult woman in mutual recognition and affirmation, because we have become prisoners in our fathers' or our husbands' houses, prisoners in the nursery, or prisoners in the marketplace! How to reunite and conquer these dividing, conquering walls?

The unconscious selfishness of fathers, husbands, lovers, or children is only reinforced by the culture we live in. Women are expected to be available to them as daughters, wives, lovers, or mothers, and we are expected to be fully four or five persons to meet all these roles with equanimity and grace. Always our charming selves. Unreal. Unpersons. Not women at all, but only the sum of our roles. We are the only ones who can put a stop to this by proclaiming the legitimate limits of our individual humanity. As for work, if the expectation to be all and give all for the job doesn't come from employers and co-workers, it often comes from ourselves. No one can fulfill such an unreasonable expectation. We end by breaking down under the impossibility of the unreal demands we've taken on from others, or made for ourselves. Meanwhile, we grieve consciously or unconsciously for having lost each other in the process. People unreeling from unreality.

I do not want to resent the men in my life for being jealous of my relationships with women. I do not want to resent children for keeping me from adult friendships with women. And I do not want to resent my work because I no longer have time to spend with the women I enjoy and care about.

I need to make my commitment to you clear to the others whom I love. They need to know that loving you takes nothing from them, but makes me more whole for them. And for my work. You are not a luxury I can take or leave, not a past love I give up with marriage or sacrifice for my career. You are necessary to me. You are an essential part of my life. We have gone through a great deal to find one another. I will not give you up or turn from you again. We do not need to be prisoners, you and I. There is an alternative. And the alternative is in ourselves. In the choices we make to remain in one another's lives literally for good—our own good and that of others.

The time has come to focus on all that unites us. We begin to be united in the knowledge that we are more than the sum of our roles. I see us in a special metamorphosis, from separation to communion, from isolation into lively union, from stifling prisoners into sister spinners. We break open the old worm sac and weave wings for ourselves. We begin to emerge with the new beauty of tropical moths and butterflies—dream unfolding before and behind our opening eyes: Swallowtail, Birdwing, Morphe awakening, no longer enclosed and contained, concentrated in the tight prison sacs of chrysalis or cocoon; finally the mighty Queen Alexandra, greatest and most sensuous of all the butterflies in the world. Freed from the pulsing prison membranes that bound them to old wood, they make their magical metamorphosis with amazing grace, their labyrinthine cells falling off like old scales from the millions of seeing eyes on their wings and bodies, tasting the fertile sweetness of creation with the fur on their feet where new tastes bud, where light is tasted as sensitively as sugar. Their wings are made of prisms. Through such fine thinness our breath passes as light passes, making more brilliance and more breathtaking color than human eye can see, each tiny cell a holy prism unto itself. From prisons to prisms, from un-mazing to amazing, from bloodless to dazzling—you and I pump the mighty living fluids into our own wet prism-wings, and I see you clearly, fully, for the first time, as you take flight.

Now for all the world to see, we are women working toward new creation, spinning and weaving the world from the silken trailings of our own unraveled lives. And we now are more than the sum of our parts together. As synergy shows the whole to be greater than

the sum of its parts, *gynergy* is the new female synergy I celebrate
with this poem:

> I have been asleep for ten years of my life
> but today am waking, waking
>
> aware of the seahorse
> alone in his quiet lair
> the male-mother who gives birth
> laboriously in salt water
>
> and aware of the male nanny grebe
> who cares for the kids
> while mother bird tests
> her wings against the sun
> for food to feed their young
>
> aware also of the countless gifts
> of female energy that would
> surely explode the world
> if they were known,
> and go wasted as if to spare
> the planet, but instead
> the planet dies with them
>
> aware of the beauty of old
> women's hands on young women's
> shoulders who take to the fluid
> process of science, paint, or poetry,
> or pound out their magic music
> on primitive drums, on strings,
> through horns sending their lusty wail:
> for life! for life!
>
> Aware of these forces I wake
> out of my middle years
> and look into the infinite
> eyes of my sisters, daughters,
> mothers, grand- and godmothers,

caught in their endless
circle of energy, created anew
in their nurture, begin to see
the vast deep roots of my woman nature
reaching around the earth and held
in their circular fire
with great white waters
running under,

and wonder, for wonder,
how I shall ever sleep again.

The spiritual spiral of female truth has metamorphosed us from girls and ladies into honest-to-Goddess women.

We are moon daughters. Our bonds are strong and subtle. We are united in a spiral of darkness and light. We do our woman's work at night, rising up, up past the precincts of the sun, and opening ourselves outward into the universe. We spin new walls of silk and gold to hold the treasures in. We are no longer separated in our common task of redeeming the holy—lost, forgotten, or abandoned. We are mothers and daughters for each other, sisters and friends, teachers and runners, swimmers and fliers, wilderness criers, singers and spinners, women weaving wondercloth from wormsilk spun with sun's gold. We weave with our own hair, worn silver and fine by time. We weave with the curled hairs of our sexual natures, with the red and gold hairs of our spiritual selves.

We are mirrors and models for each other. Now I dare to see myself in you and you in myself, and I delight in knowing us both to be greater and less than I feared.

. We are myth-makers and dream-sharers. We tell stories, spin truths out of dream flax, reveal secrets, become friends. We teach each other new generosity. We plan and build new lives, new dreams, and we make new names for ourselves. We read each other's books and make poems collectively and thank the Mother God for the healing gift of passionate friendships and the easy pleasure of casual bonds of experience and trust. We draw courage from each other in the spiritual intimacy of spinning separate pasts and futures into a shared present. In short, we celebrate ourselves.

But do not forget, and do not let me forget, how we got here.

Do not forget, and do not let me forget, that what we have found in each other is a new discovery, powerful and fragile, not to be grasped ungratefully, never to be taken for granted. We will surely fall back into the old ways, plant ourselves back on the old wood, and spin new cocoons for ourselves. We will fail again. We will lose each other. But now we know that we can always come back, we can always spin our way back to each other, break through wet and dry walls, and climb out into the sun on our own threads.

I leave you now with this gift. It is a prayerpoem my friend Pesha made and gave to me. She would want me to pass it on to you:

> I am one with the Earth Mother
> I am one with the Sky Queen
>
> It is my heritage to walk on the earth
> and to soar beyond the furthest stars
>
> My mother is the trees
> My mother is the moon
>
> My mother is you, my sister
> and my mother is me.

CHAPTER 3
LOVING MEN

Starchildren

Starchildren, born in a tight clenched mass,
wet, small, a tiny ball of screaming fear
imploded in birth

our lives meant to grow open,
explode, embrace life's gift,
we human flowers told by earth
UNCLENCH YOURSELF!
clench tighter till we burst or wither,
wasted with a love held in, suffocated.

Now I say to you, my Friend,
one life calling to another,
Unclench yourself, Unclench yourself

so I can love you in the open
under sun and sky, on warm wet grass,
the jewelled ocean coming toward us,
Yes! Yes!

29

I'll be your friend, won't clench or close you,
hold you close with open arms, I'll love you.

Dear Other, Dear Brother,

There is so much I have to say to you. Our relationship has always been so complicated. The obstacles to love between us are overwhelming. Sometimes I feel overwhelmed by the contradictions of your wants, and sometimes by the contradictions of my own toward you. Both of us have turned from each other in despair more than once over the burdens of expectation that neither of us wanted, but were taught by society to bear toward each other, and toward ourselves.

I want to speak to you about my own despair in loving you or being loved by you, and about my wishes and longings to love you well and be truly loved by you.

How many times has love been displaced between us by power pretending to be love? How many times have I failed you by not being for you what only your father could be? How often has your longing for him been displaced onto me, ironically? And you have failed me in being a mother to me. Truly we fail each other whenever we try to make each other over into the image of someone else. I cannot be your father. You will not be free to love me until you and he are loving toward each other. The reverse is not always true. You have often been a mother to me—given me the closeness I've had before only with my own mother, the time, the tenderness, the care, the feeding. But I have been so unfair to you in longing for my mother in you. Loving other women and loving myself frees me to love you not for my mother in you, but for yourself.

It's been said that people of both sexes seek their mothers in their mates. Perhaps in our culture this has some truth. The first conflict in life is our contradictory need to be reunited with our mothers, and to separate ourselves from them. You and I play out this conflict over and over, with infantile precision. We cry out toward one another from opposite corners, "Take care of me!" And we leave each other alone or punish each other for being needy instead of all-giving.

I do not want to be your mother or your daughter. I do not want you to be a perpetually dependent little boy or me a perpetually dependent little girl. What I learned in loving women I now want with you as well: I want us to be free to give and receive support, care, and loving tenderness from each other, always mindful of the innate dignity and individuality of the other. We can be sister and brother, and even mother or father for each other, but we can never again, my Love, take away from the other's human dignity and freedom, or we will be sent back to the corners we deserve, alone and unhappy.

I am more aware of your old dependency on me because it strikes deeper in many ways than my dependency on you. Women have been so brutally dependent on men for money and security. You have depended on us for sexual and emotional comfort. Society has created a macho ethic to encourage you to acquire wealth and power in order to impress me. Have you noticed that I am no longer impressed? And do you really impress each other, or do you show each other the grief and longing for tenderness between you as men that for so long you admitted only to me? As for me, I am tired of being only a comforting body for you. I want to be able to meet you fully as the powerful and needy woman I am, the spiritual and physical reality of my own humanity fully present and appreciated.

A few years ago I spinned the frayed ends of my longing for this honesty between us into the threads of a poem which I called *Travail:*

> We women bear men
> even though they cannot bear us.
> We bear them over and over
> as fathers, sons, and lovers.
>
> May this ill-bearing end.
> May they enter the Cosmic Womb
> of the Great Mother and be
> well-born by Her once and forever.

May they emerge as our brothers
and may we their mothers
become only their sisters and lovers.

I do not know if returning to the Motherhood of God will set you free, or returning to the lost parenting you crave from your father will set you free, or if you can do both of these for yourself. I wish freeing and healing for you. I am truly eager to meet you also as a whole person, a human being who has reclaimed his own dignity and neediness and is able to take responsibility for himself.

Now I will tell you what has interfered between us.

Do you know the story of Ariadne and Theseus? Ariadne was a princess of Crete in ancient times. According to legend, Crete was the seat of the famous Labyrinth, which housed the Minotaur. This monster was the child of an unholy union—its mother was human and its father was a bull. The Minotaur had the body of a man and the head of a bull. Each year, fourteen youths were sent from Athens to be sacrificed as food for the Minotaur. One year a young man named Theseus was among the fourteen. When Ariadne saw him she fell in love with him. She promised to save him if he would agree to marry her and take her away with him. He gave her his pledge. Before he entered the deadly Labyrinth, Ariadne gave Theseus a ball of golden thread which had been spun by Daedalus, the builder of the Labyrinth. He unwound it as he moved more deeply into the Maze, and Ariadne held one end of it outside so that he could find his way back to her and freedom. When he reached the place where the beast awaited him, he took the sword which Ariadne had given him and pierced the Minotaur as she had instructed. Then he followed the golden thread to find his way out of the Maze. Ariadne took him to the ships of the Athenians who were waiting. Together they set sail. They stopped at an island to rest on their way. As Ariadne slept, Theseus and the Athenians stole away. When she awakened, it was only to discover that she had been abandoned. Some legends say she later became the bride of Dionysus and mother of many children. Others say she died alone on the island and when Theseus finally returned for her, he grieved. She was given divine honors.

I recognize myself in the myth. I have tried to bribe you into being my savior, into liberating me from my narrow, sheltered life and replacing the security my father provided with excitement and wealth. I have wanted you to be my knight, my valiant lover, my dashing hero. I have wanted to make you into a little Father God or Godfather, and I have been willing to forfeit my own self-respect by playing out the role of fairy princess to please you. But you knew it was too much. You knew I had what you needed, and you were ready to try to live out the romantic lie in order to save your own life. You used me to slay the monster in yourself, and I allowed this, knowing you couldn't do it alone. I used your doom and entrapment to win my own freedom. But both of us lost. You condemned yourself to a life of solitude, and my would-be freedom was more confining than the Maze.

In becoming your savior I forfeited my freedom. In becoming my savior you doomed yourself to failure. In the end we were both alone with our grief and guilt. The truth is that you are the only one who can save yourself, and I am the only one who can free myself.

You are the only one who can confront the beast that is half-human with the head of a bull. We call some people bull-headed. Perhaps this is the part of a person that rushes head-on into war and blood-lust, into ambition toward riches and power over others, the part that is forever cut off from the human heart. Perhaps you fear that without my help you will be powerless against this beast, overcome and devoured. I will help you, my Brother, by encouraging you to meet the beast and call it by name, to own it and tame it, to teach it more humane ways. But I will not forfeit myself or take what is yours away from you by holding you to false promises or doing the task for you. There is an alternative to my desperation.

I am the only one who can build the boat that will free me from the small world of this imprisoning island of my Self. I can save us both from the lie of the princess and the knight if I work toward my freedom in direct and practical ways. Living this lie for years has condemned us both to false roles which make us despise ourselves and each other in the end.

The cowardice of Theseus in his abandonment of the sleeping Ariadne has given men the reputation of untrustworthy users of women. We are placed in the false position of giving our bodies as if they were sacred hosts, only to be trampled on by men who seem ungrateful and have become as Vampire Lovers in our eyes, taking not only our bodies, but feeding on our blood as well. Because the giving and the taking become one-sided, women fit the mold of victims and men are cast as taking and raping. Such is the language of nightmares and legends which are formed out of bitter human disappointments. The reality is usually not so grotesque, but it is still horribly painful. We have created false roles for each other and the only outcome to such foolishness is betrayal.

You, my once bright knight, fall in my eyes. I take your plain human cowardice for elaborate, inhuman cruelty. You are not the all-providing father, or if you are, you are not the tender and exciting lover of my dreams, and I declare you wretched in my sight. Yet the *No Trespassing* sign over your heart still galls and wounds me.

I, your saving princess, fall asleep and reveal myself to be merely mortal. You begin to see my weakness as repulsive. My giving deteriorates into ugly martyrdom. You begin to despise me as one despises self-made victims. You feel I am a more dangerous threat to you than the Labyrinth you escaped, and you flee to save yourself from becoming entangled in my subtle but insistent pull into a web of commitment.

All the time you must fight against my pressure to make you heroic, all-capable, all-providing, all-caring, and inhuman. This is not easy for you, since our culture also presses you to be these things. Yet the culture and I insult you by forever reminding you that you are only ridiculous in your attempts to be the impossible! How you must despair. Why don't we all go mad?

I feel the pressures of pretending to be what I am not: the saving image of your own soul, the caged goddess of your longings, the Perfect Mother, all-giving lover, synthetically beautiful, endlessly nurturing, the Mama, the Mermaid, the Prostitute, or the honorary male let in the men's club by right of my spunk and intelligence.

The trap of being your mother is that you will resent me for being a human being working side by side with you in the marketplace, for the unforgivable sin of mothers is that they compete with their sons. As a mother I should only sacrifice myself to enhance you, but sacrifice is unattractive and mothers are the bane of their children's life when sacrifice has the high price of guilt attached to it.

The trap of being your soul-image is that this too makes me inhuman. Being *super*human is not better than being *sub*human for one who is *human*. You cannot obtain your spiritual salvation through me either, any more than I can obtain my mortal salvation through you. The myth of the Mermaid shows this. The fantasy of the beautiful creature who is half woman with the tail of a fish, who lives in the sea, who mates with a man—and loses herself. I know human women who try to live out this fantasy to please their men. One woman drew the image of cutting off her tail to be more lovely, but then she could neither walk nor swim. The Mermaid is immobile in human terms. She is captive. She is kept from the mainstream of human life and is always dependent. But in growing out of her tail, the fish-woman becomes whole-woman. With a woman's feet and legs she can both walk and swim, unlike her webbed sister who lives only in the sea of some men's minds. Do not make me your Mermaid, because I will not live down to her limitations. Making love with such a creature cannot be very fulfilling!

And the Prostitute. What keeps me in this last mythic role? My fear of poverty. My fear of solitude. My fear for the well-being of my children. Simple economic dependence. And the pity elicited by your sexual despair that unless I love you, no one will. This last appeals to my ego, of course. My false vanity. My image of myself as the Great Lover. The only one who can save you. But I am not

Ariadne. I do not have the golden thread, even in the splendors of my sexual gifts. They will not help you in the long run to find yourself . . . and to find me. I do not have to be chained to you by the treasures of the flesh, giving you the illusion that you are worshipped by a woman, and giving me the fool's gold of material goods to the ruin of my own soul through loss of myself. Loss of self-respect and mounting resentment toward you. Surely the price of the lie has risen too high. Surely we owe each other the truth, now, finally.

I cannot love you while I am trapped in these false roles, and you cannot love me trapped in yours. If I am Mother, Mermaid, and Prostitute, you must be Child, Lecher, and Pimp. We have created a myth in which we are doomed to hate each other in the end for the steady sapping away of our humanity. The reality of this illusion is more trapping and more deadly to us both than the Minotaur lurking in the Labyrinth was to the fourteen young men and women whose flesh kept him alive each year.

We owe each other profound apology, profound forgiveness. We must pass through the death of our illusions, fears, dependencies, and guilt, in order to restore whatever innocent, truthful, and lifegiving love there was once between us:

> We have been born together
> many times before,
> giving life to each other
> from our own innocent bodies;
>
> this time we have died together
> and can only be borne
> from one another's wounds.

Loving you has been so dangerous for me, because it seemed I had to lose the love of myself for you. I had to love you more than myself to love you at all. This was nothing less than self-mutilation. Giving up my body and my soul for an unfulfilling love, because how could you fully love someone who wasn't really there? I want to rise from the wounds of my self-mutilation and grow whole with you.

But I am still a bit afraid of you. I want to see you rise from your own wounds and heal yourself. I know now that I can only love you and have your love if I love myself fully, and the same is true of you. I do not have to give up my freedom or my self-respect or my Self to love you, and if I have in the past, it has not been for love, but for love's sham. I have dishonored both of us by offering you less than a whole woman, and you have dishonored both of us by taking less. Were you afraid of me because I am Other? You yourself found me within your own soul, recreated according to your desires. Perhaps I am not so Other after all. And perhaps our fear of one another has made us both seem more Other than we are. I am not the image of Woman you created within you and projected onto me, nor are you the image of Man I created. We are neither of us as powerful or as fragile as we imagine.

We both have within us the capacity for kindness, appreciation, and respect which we both crave. Whether you are my father, brother, son, or lover, whether you are my friend, acquaintance, or co-worker, I have the human right to expect kindness, appreciation, and respect from you. I have the human right not to be patronized or tolerated, not to be ridiculed or condemned. By now you know that I cannot be confined within the kitchen, nursery, or bedroom. The world needs the gifts of my intelligence, stamina, and daring as much as my creativity, nurturing, and affection. And my human need is to give these things to the world, and like you, to be recognized. Yes, we are competitors of a sort, but competitors may be friendly and cooperative, and may stimulate one another toward self-improvement in mutual congeniality. Competitors need not be rivals; they may be true comrades. I desire to be your comrade in creating a better world. This is as much a loving desire as my desire to be your sister, friend, or lover.

There is one aspect of work which still is a source of pain to me. I do not follow the male models of work. I do not worship work. I do not place it above all things, above God, above love, above people, above myself. I have seen you so frantic or so single-minded about your work that it comes before everything else in your life.

It even comes before me. Perhaps this is because of all the social messages which encourage you to identify work with success, and success with self-worth. Your ego is in your work and not in the rest of your life. But work is no substitute for life. It is only a part of your life. Sometimes I feel that you try to prove yourself in relationships just as you have had to prove yourself in work. This tends to be destructive. I do not want to fall into this trap myself. I do not want you to be hurt by it any more. I want you to take pride in your work, as I do in mine, but I do not want you to define yourself and your worth only in terms of your work. Above all, I honestly do not want always to be placed last. I do not want you always to put the importance of your work before the importance of our relationship. Material security is no substitute for your loving presence. If you are a father or a spouse, what good are you to your family if you sacrifice yourself upon the altar of your job and leave your loved ones in an early death, or without having taken the time to show them your love? Your job has for too long been the curse of Job to your loved ones. It costs you your life in ways you do not even see. You do not notice that your sons and daughters are lost to you, that your possessions are wasted and useless, your life is being destroyed. And like Job, you do not listen to your friends. Listen to me, now, my Friend. I want you well and alive. And selfishly I want more from you than material gifts and gratitude; I want your graceful presence, your care, your contentment in a life together with others. I will not let you abandon me in new and destructive ways, dear Brother, dear Love.

What are some of the other conflicts in our companionship? The conflict between Love and Freedom, between Love and Fear, between Love and Guilt; the conflicts of Love and Jealousy, Love and Resentment, Love and Dishonesty. And the ever-present war between dependence and independence. We cannot rid ourselves of these tensions, but we can live with them honestly and courageously.

Many of these conflicts for me center around the problem that I have looked at with you from several angles: that in loving you

I have risked losing myself; that so much of my self-love, or what passed for self-love, in the past depended on your . . . not love, but approval. If only you had really loved me instead of merely approved of me! Now I must achieve some sense of self-worth, some noble independence through not needing your approval, but wanting your love. It is a more free thing to want than to need. I want you. I do not need you so much anymore, but don't be frightened by this: the less bound I am by needing you, the freer I am to love you. Use follows need; love follows want. In the past, both of us cared more about you than about me, because we live in a world that values males and devalues females, but by the grace of God and a few wise and brave women and men, the world and you and I are changing. We are learning to care about one another equally. We may even occasionally put me first! (Forgive me. This is still very difficult for me even to suggest. You must take me seriously, even if I jest.)

How hard it's been for me to be honest with you, or with myself about my feelings toward you. Usually in the past I felt so guilty about any negative feelings toward you that I completely denied them. The misery of that is that it doesn't work. The denial of guilt and the denial of the guilt-making feelings only build an unwanted resentment in me toward you that is bound to come up in subtle and destructive ways.

I have spent years cultivating emotional dishonesty as a virtue, deceiving myself into thinking I was protecting you from being hurt by my real feelings, when in reality I have punished you unfairly by thousands of indirect, nearly unnoticeable attacks which accomplish no improvement in our mutual understanding. How painfully I am learning to be simple, direct, and honest. How frightening it is to me to reveal my own anger or impatience or sense of injustice to myself. I've given you so little credit for being reasonable and strong enough to participate in honest growth-producing dialogue with me. Your own sense of self-worth is new enough that I am not always confident that you will listen to me undefensively, or that you will hear me at all. Worse than this for me is that I've given myself little or no credit for having a valid position if a complaint in our relationship should arise from either of us! We both still need so much affirmation from each other. The best affirmation is in being heard, and in being met. Love and anger are not the killing opponents that love and fear are. I am learning to love you enough not to be afraid of you, or of your rejection, and to entrust you with my anger. The expression of legitimate anger can be as much a gift as the expression of genuine affection, and it requires at least as much esteem for oneself and for the other as any other act of trust.

What of that other separating monster, jealousy? It's so easy for men and women to be jealous of anything that claims the other's time and love: work, children, even ideals. Sexual rivals are only the most blatant objects of jealousy. When we are jealous, we feel betrayed and cheated; cheated because someone or something else has what we do not have, and what we very much want; and betrayed because the myth of perfect union with another is shattered every time that longed-for other turns away from us for any reason. The way beyond jealousy—which is always a sign of great longing being frustrated—is to provide oneself what we had too narrowly demanded from another. If I can give to myself what I had counted only on you to give me, I will free myself from the negative form of dependence inherent in jealousy, and I will free you at the same time to give to me not out of compulsion, but the simple desire to give. Such freedom and independence are not the enemies of love —they are love's wings. If I find wholeness and union within myself, I will not bleed you of your humanity by demanding that you lose your individual separateness in the symbiotic bliss of our union. I will allow you to express your love for me with natural generosity and spontaneity. If I do not destroy jealousy in this way, it will destroy our love by displacing it with bondage and the tyranny of suspicion and expectation.

Envy is the negative twin of jealousy. Jealousy feels threatened by what you do or what you love away from me, and envy feels threatened by what you have that I do not have. If I come to value what I do have, and see that it is of equal importance to your possessions or gifts, though different from yours, then I will free myself to rejoice with you in what you own.

Freedom is related to Agape—the love that lets be. Love begins
with delight in the being of the beloved; love often ends when the
freedom of the loved one has been destroyed and delight turns to
disgust. Agape is the quality of love that stands for and preserves
the freedom of the other, even when that freedom is in conflict with
one's own self-interest. My Agape toward you allows me to desire
your well-being, even more than my own pleasure. It is the gift that
enables us to make sacrifices for each other so easily and graciously
that we don't even know we're doing it. The extreme expression
of Agape would be in loving you with such intense desire for your
well-being that I would be willing to give you up, to let you go if being
with me in any way conflicted with your being well. Once in my life,
Agape made such a demand of me. Once is all I could bear in a life-
time. From this experience I learned that while freedom may sometimes be in conflict with Eros —the quality of love that longs for
union— it can never conflict with Agape. As Eros is the servant of
Agape, freedom is the servant of love. As Eros curdles without
Agape and ceases to be a quality of love, freedom sours without love
and ceases to be a blessing. Agape is also hollow without Eros, as
love is impossible without freedom. If I cannot fly with you, my love,
I would far rather see you fly alone—or with another—than not to
fly at all.

Agape

To desire
your well-being
more than
our being together.

Eros

To desire
our well-being
by our being
together.

That time I let you go—I remember how my being rebelled, the
depths of bottomless pain I felt at first, as if I had pulled out my heart

and thrown it in the fire. And then, slowly, slowly, the buoyancy
began, the rising lightness, and finally, my own ability to fly again,
freer, more brilliantly than before. In freeing you I freed myself.
Then I rejoiced in the gift we had in one another, the reality of love
between us that not even time and space could diminish. Our love
was like marrow to me: "the soft, vascular, fatty tissue that fills the
cavities of most bones; the innermost, essential, or choicest part;
pith; vitality."

Marrow

My flesh knows you,
knows you in ways you
do not know yourself,
and knows itself because of you.

Surprising it still appalls me
to know strangers give flesh
to each other
when what we gave was between
lovers who've shared life
to our souls' marrow.

The marrow of the bone is bitter,
being too close to light and air.
Darkness gives the deep soft insides
of the larger being its peculiar sweetness.
It was this we tasted of each other.
The marrow of the bone can be betrayed.
The deeper marrow bears no lying.

Lovers and givers we neither
of us knew beyond the moment
what it would be like
to fulfill the endless longing
in the other to be loved and given unto
eternally, eternally, unconditionally
loved and worthy of it.

But your flesh knows me
and my flesh loves you for it.
We end as we began,
insatiable, unsatisfied, afraid,
but knowing now the one thing
we could not know then—

I cannot say what that thing is,
but that it changed me
beyond all knowing of myself,
aged and made me young,
broke and saved me, and that
you, too, are not the same.

Finally, I have stopped looking toward you for my own completion. I have stopped pouring myself into you to save and complete you. I am ready simply to meet you, ready for both of us to become complete in the meeting, not in each other. I am woman, whole unto myself, no one's possession. You are man, and the same. I free myself to complete myself. You do the same. When we meet, I will not be perfect for you, and you will not be perfect for me, but we may be complete as we have never been before. Before, when I lost myself in you, I let myself forget that the losing is only good in the finding. I forgot to find myself. And you never lost yourself in me for more than the thin moment of ecstasy when we made love. I will let myself be found, and you may let yourself become lost, and we both can teach each other something new.

When either of us was possessive toward the other, each of us became an adversary, resisting the imagined threat of abandonment or bondage: we became Beloved Enemy, each to each. Oh, my Love, let us turn ourselves around and discover in the other the miracle of a Friendly Lover!

I pray the Love Mantra to set us both free to find each other again:

Love Mantra for Letting Go

I bless you
I release you

> I set you free
> I set me free
>
> I let you be
> I let me be

I still have Eros toward you, as the sometimes frightening, sometimes beloved Other. I desire to be with you not as one, but as two together. I am ready for the renewed challenge of growing into greater fullness of being because you and I are on this planet together, and because the alternative to our oppression of each other is in our willingness to grow as individuals together in the most delicate, most difficult, most dangerous, most potentially delightful of all human relationships:

> To grow young with you now
> out of our rigid youth
> in middle years, our bodies
> open to each other,
> the flesh more rugged,
> soft, fragile, sensitive
> to a hair's kiss,
> our faces lined with a fine suffering
> wrought from years of weathering love.
>
> We grow young, we grow wise
> in our bodies' breath,
> rounder than before,
> thinner, braver,
> laughing incandescent,
> senile in our skins,
> eager to grow and grow
> old together, loving all the way.

Then, in the renewing fulfillment of our loving, the oneness *between* us will have *a creative life of its own*, perpetually pregnant with vitality and peace:

Heart Seed

Put your hand here,
husband of my heart,
and feel the life
you create in me.
So deep, so deep comes
your seed inside me
in our loving that you
impregnate not my womb
but my heart, husband—
see how it opens,
fills and grows, eager
to create life in you,
to carry us as one
into the world anew . . .

CHAPTER 4
LOVING CHILDREN

Dear Daughters, Dear Sons,

Do you wonder why I never had you? My beloved, unborn children, I've carried you in my body for thirty years. Now I am going to tell you why I have chosen not to have you.

Isn't that a funny way of saying it—"having" children? Whether you are born or not, you could never belong to me. And one of the first things I would teach you is that you must not let yourselves be "had" by anyone. Being had is being halved.

I understand something about children needing to be born and raised in freedom because of the poem-children that come into the world through me. Like you, they live unformed in the limbo of my body and soul. I love them into being, as I would love you into being. They draw their life from my life, as you would. But they are not me. They are not even mine. They exist unto themselves. It is my honor to help them form themselves and unfold themselves into the world. In a sense, I give them to the world, as I would give you, but they are gifts, not possessions, not even extensions of myself. I honor them as beings in their own right, as I would honor you.

This doesn't mean that I am not responsible to these new creatures as they take their being. The bond between my poems and me
is more than a spirit-bond—it is a blood-bond, as truly as the bond
between you and me would be. They draw from my blood, as you
would. They sing in my bones, as you would. I shed blood in birthing them, as I would for you. Because their words are organs from
my own flesh, I will always be bound to care for them, as I would
for you, but never to draw them back into myself, for that would
only kill them, and destroy me. They are living things, as you would
be, and living things must be free to move and grow and be according to their own unique design.

Do you think I never birthed you because I was always too busy
making poems? No. Many women are poets or scholars or doctors
or carpenters or lawyers or bankers or singers or priests or scientists, and also mothers, as many men are fathers. But being a human
parent is a very special vocation, an awesome responsibility, a test
of endurance, patience, wisdom, and humor. I admire this vocation
in those who have it, and I am saddened when I see people who
don't have it going ahead and making, then failing their children,
as if just anyone could be a good parent.

Unfortunately, too many humans forget that they are different
from the other animals. Just because they have the biological equip-
ment for making babies, they go ahead and bring children into the
world as irresponsibly as some cats do. If they don't know how to
care for them, teach them, feed them, help them, listen to them,
learn from them, or love them—too bad. I think that having babies
who are human requires a great deal more than many humans have
to give. It requires intelligence, patience, time, skill, flexibility, good
will, loving kindness, stamina, endurance, fun-lovingness, and most
of all, a strong desire to do the tasks of parenting in order to nurture another human being into well-being on this planet and in the
universe. Now, my dears, that's an awe-full lot. My women-friends
who are mothers tell me how inadequate they feel after their children are born. I simply feel inadequate before the fact. The limits
of my personality, body, and soul, and the boundaries of my choices

for my own life honestly do not add up to parenthood. I do not have a vocation to be your mother at this time in my life. And since the planet is already overpopulated, I am under no moral obligation to let you in through my body.

I do not feel guilty toward you, as I might if I yielded to external pressures and the expectations of others, and then knew that I had made an irreversible mistake by (excuse me) having you. In fact, I can think of several people I know whose friends might be better off if their mothers had practiced contraception! Nearly every mother at one time or another considers the benefits of retroactive birth control—but this doesn't mean that her children are unwanted on the whole, just on certain days. Parenting isn't easy!

I know it won't hurt you to hear this in your present amorphous state, so I will tell you quite honestly that I don't want you. I may want you someday, but I don't want you now. And my reasons for not wanting you are as selfish and as unselfish as another woman's reasons for wanting her children might be. Selfish, because I know my great need for solitude, for quiet, for the beauty of an ordered and serene environment. My work requires me to nurture others through the day. It is in withdrawing into the silence of my harmonious home that I am given the means to restore inner harmony, to be nurtured in my nest, to find peace in the inner environment and get my soul's tank filled for the next day. I am protective of this, because it is necessary to my ministry, to my well-being, as well as to my being with others in a healing way. This is the reality of my temperamental need. Unselfish, because I know that I should become frustrated by your childlike need for my time and attention, which you truly deserve. I should feel guilty and then resentful toward you for being a source of my guilt and sense of inadequacy—and I do not want resentment to be a condition of our bond. You deserve more of me than I feel able to give you. I respect your needs, your right to be noisy, to be disorderly, to be attended. I would wish for you all the time and space for these things that I believe you deserve and need. If you had ten parents besides your father and me to support your discovery of the world, and if you had your own house to be the laboratory for that discovery, I would feel more confident in inviting you here. Such is the limit and perhaps the weakness of my idealism. Only the kibbutz movement approaches the reality of what I feel I would need to bring you into physical life, and there are no such places nearby. There you have it, my children.

As much as possible, I don't want to cheat either of us. Another woman might decide to bear children for precisely this same reason that has made me decide not to. Today, thank God, we have this freedom.

Now that I've told you this, I'd like to go ahead and speak to you in a "let's pretend" way, as if I were going to give birth to you. I'd like to tell you what my wishes would be for my daughters and sons.

First, I'll speak to you, my daughters. I have such mixed feelings toward you. I am afraid for you, coming into an alien world—a world doubly alien to you as females. But I am proud to bear you, proud to see you grow into strong, wise, free, and loving women. My girl-children, I will teach you from the first moment that you are capable of greatness, that you are lovable and worthy of the best. You will have trouble. Others will tell you different things about yourself. They will not see your strength or acknowledge your intelligence. But I will always tell you the truth about yourself: that you are a whole human being, a normal person filled with normal contradictions, and that *you are all right*.

Daughters, hold your heads high, aim for the stars. Believe in your power to think, to move, to create, to change the world, to love, to feel, to hurt, to heal, to be. Let no one take being from you. Let no one lessen you. Let no one tame you. You were born free, and my love for you is a love that wishes your freedom. Life will bind you. Life will also stretch you. This is life's contradiction. You will die both bound and free. But do not forget that freedom was your birthright.

Do not worry. I will also let you be weak with me. I will not tell you "You can take care of yourself," and then leave you alone. I will care for you, hold you, cradle and nurse you—but only when you want me to. I will not violate your dignity. And I will keep to this pledge all your life, to care for and to respect you, in your neediness, and in your freedom and strength.

Live honestly and passionately. Love your life. Live boldly. Enjoy. Love and enjoy your own womanly body. Cherish its rhythms and changes. Delight in your whole physical reality. Do not be ashamed of your sexuality or your muscular ability to play, love, run, dance, compete, or work. Beauty and strength are in you together. You are made in the image of God, female. Celebrate.

And you, my sons. I am glad to have sons in order to place men on this planet who will truly love women and honor their dignity and freedom. I fear for you, too, because others will teach you to fear women, and to hate yourself. I want you to grow to love your own humanity, all of it— its tenderness, its neediness, its weakness and vulnerability, its true beauty and grace, its natural capability and self-givingness, its completion and incompletion. When you truly love yourself, you will be free to love women. The fear that you have of yourself need not be projected onto women. Own it. Overcome it, with help from others.

I will not hold you to myself and suffocate you. I will not make you small or puff you up. I will love you honestly and with open arms.

My sons, above all things be loving and love your own feeling nature. Let go of whatever bulliness others may try to put on you. It will hurt you and keep away your loved ones. Know that you are free to feel, to entrust the beauty, strength, and fragility of your feelings to others, to women and to men. Love your own body and do not fear it. When you meet the body of a woman, cherish her in her flesh as you cherish yourself. Hear and honor her feelings and her intelligence as you honor your own.

As you learn to enjoy deeper intimacy, stay strong and free as well. Do not forfeit your deep manliness, but simply discover your dimensions of complexity. Be both tender and wild! Run on the earth and swim the seas and be powerful in the pure pleasure of your man-flesh. You, also, are created in God's image, as magnetically compelling in all the fires and winds of cosmos. Rejoice in your being.

My daughters and my sons, beloved children of my body, I will love you and I will let you go into the world in the freedom of your own being. I entrust you to yourselves, and to those you choose in life to be your friends and lovers . . .

My unborn children, I do not want you now. I may want you some-day. Or I may want to adopt grandchildren when I am old and my own life well-lived. Meanwhile, I will respect your image as I recognize it in other children. I will listen and learn from them what you might teach me if you were here. And I will be loyal to the children of my soul that I bring into being in my life and work—ideas, poems, books, relationships—all the new beings that can come forth from my being, creating themselves from the flesh of my flesh and the soul of my soul.

I will seek wisdom and grace in loving those who come into my life as children needing nurture, and I will give them the same respect and freedom that I would give you. I will not keep them children in order to make myself feel needed and useful. I will encourage them to grow themselves into interdependent adulthood, and I will let them go in order to meet them anew as equals.

Dear children, I am amazed at what you have taught me without even having been born. I will not forget you. I will go on listening and learning from you. And I may teach you something as well. You are the mythic children of timelessness. You may have a freedom mere human children don't have, to speak to other mothers and fathers, sons and daughters. You carry possibility with you. Help those of us who are mortal to grow more humane in all our creating, birthing, and parenting.

> I may see your faces in others, or in eternity.
> Thank you for not being, and for being in your own way.
> I will always love you.

CHAPTER 5
THE OTHER SIDE OF LOVE

Dear Flesh of My Flesh and Soul of My Soul,

I am dreaming you into myself. You are all the images of possibility and longing within me. You came with me from eternity. You were born with my being. You live in my flesh and spin dreams in my soul. You are all the women and men longing for love within me. You are all the frightened children within me. You are afraid to look at yourselves.

Do not be afraid now. I will show you your images within my dreaming. I will not turn you away.

How far you are from the youth Narcissus who was so enchanted with his own image that, gazing at it in the watery pool, he fell into it and drowned! You have never even seen your own image. You have never dared to look. Look now. Your danger is not in being held and compelled, falling and drowning into yourself, but in hiding from and forever losing your Self. Your purpose is to unclench, unfold, unmask; to spin into the world of reality and wonder, to weave truth through human lives and redeem them. Look.

In my dream, I cross a bridge that spans a stream. I am standing in a clearing in a forest. Before me there is an old majestic tree. In front of the tree I see an enormous butterfly, beating its wings at great speed, but blending motion with perfect stillness. It stays there, near the top of the tree's trunk, suspended in midair. I am in awe, and move closer to see better. Now I realize that the breathtaking creature is two creatures mating. They are birds or butterfly birds, six feet wide with their wings spread, their slender bodies joined in the middle. This is perfect union, their gold and orange, white and black rimmed wings beating in rhythm, their bodies humming. The golden wings of birds mating in midair. "So that's how they do it," I say in my dream.

Of course, this isn't the way birds or butterflies mate in the waking world. But in the sleep world of All Possibility, any wonderful thing can happen. What I saw was completion, wholeness, ecstasy of union, two beings weaving themselves together on a spun thread of invisible steel. Miracle. Blessedness. I had the feeling of being in a holy place where neither shoes nor clothes are needed. A place simply to be. And a place to find the beloved other. A meeting place. A place of unhindered coming together. The ecstatic presence of the winged beings in union had the shape of a glittering web, vibrating at fantastic pitch, silk strings singing pure notes from loving bodies and prism-sparkling wings. I knew those beings to be you. I recognized in my dream the fulfilled image of all longing, all yearning, all possibility for joy and ecstasy in completed being. The loving creatures gave beauty as you can give, in the redeeming act of loving and being loved. This is the moment stopping time for which you and I were born.

It is the moment we have so often lost.

It is the moment in which we still can be found.

We must prepare to give ourselves to the possibility of love. We come to the final unlayering of ourselves, to peel off the last onion-thin skin and see the last defeating barriers to love within ourselves, and weep and be cleansed.

We were born for ecstasy. We were not born for pain. We were born to love, not to suffer. But the way to love is painful according to the barriers against love which must be broken. Love endures in the form of longing. Ecstasy breaks through only momentarily, rarely, and is transforming, for it draws us out of ourselves, to meet, like the mating butterflies, in the mid-space between ourselves, and to be changed in the meeting. Ecstasy is not love's goal, but its blinding surprise. It may come only once in a life-time. It is a preparation for death. It is the miracle of being able to live beyond oneself. It blinds and reveals all.

I know from my own experience and from others who have told me they have felt the same that there are paradoxical moments in making love when the two come closest to losing themselves in each other in simultaneous orgasm, and are at the same time heartbroken with the awareness of remaining two. In the very moment of most intense intimacy, the ultimate loneliness of being human breaks through and overwhelms the lovers. The impossibility of perfect union appears just as the fusion of two into one takes place.

Because love exists to enhance, not destroy being, the simultaneous ecstasy and despair of love is that two can never remain as one. For this to happen, both would die. Love gives us brief moments of seeming to know what it would be like to die and to be reborn in another, in the beloved, and these moments are the ecstatic seconds, the climaxes of life when lovers do experience themselves to die and live again inside each other. If the moments lasted for any duration, the lovers would actually die. The love between them calls them into more life, not death, and so love sends them back to themselves, and to the loneliness of separateness. We remain separated by our skin, by our distinctive and unique individuality. Yet the separation itself is a kind of blessedness, for it allows us to touch, to kiss, to speak, to hold one another, to enhance one another, and this would not be possible if the two remained as one. Instead of lasting union, what love bestows between persons is completion. The illusion of perfection gives way to the reality of completion in love. The longing for union, for transformation with another, is not fulfilled deeply when two disappear into one which is neither, but a transcendent third—the personification of love as Angel, present during the eternal seconds of spiritual or physical orgasm—and neither is it fulfilled—but rather more cruelly frustrated—when one person disappears into the other. Rather, this longing is most deeply fulfilled as two move purely together; the purity of movement is itself the full-filling gift.

What within us interferes with our ability to move purely together as two completions?

Life is infinite longing crippled by fear. Perfect love casts out fear—but since love is never perfect in this life, fear remains. When a relationship brings two together in completion and transformation, their beings move together refined by complexity. Completion uses complexity like the alchemist's essences, to turn dross into gold. Completion contains and uses fear, but fear remains. I know that in myself fear can be more compelling than love, even strongly felt love. My will to love is sabotaged by the will of fear within me to incarcerate me within myself. Instead of being incarnated in my flesh, love remains incarcerated in my hidden cells, and I remain lost to myself. What I fear to face within myself is the greatest obstacle to my ability to be, in love.

> Being in love means
> having to give and being
> free to receive.

I am not free to receive so long as I deny my need to receive. I lie to myself, telling myself that it's more important for me to love than to be loved, that being unloved doesn't hurt. The truth is that it's equally important to be loved and to love. My fear to admit this is my fear of the pain of not being loved.

I have been taught to define myself as a sacrificer, a servant, a lover and giver. But I also want to be loved and given unto, to believe that I am worthy of being served and sacrificed for. *I want to be loved and given unto unconditionally.* There is no reinforcement for this need in me, and if I dare to look at it, I recoil in guilt. I despair of it ever being fulfilled. I turn from it, deny it, go on pretending that loving is enough.

Do I have the courage to look, to face the infinite yearning within me to be loved? There is so little help from the outside. Women and religious men in our culture have been taught only to give, not to receive; only to love others, not ourselves. How can we love others without loving ourselves first, as beloved children of God, created in the image of the Holy One? "Love your neighbor as yourself," not the other way around. And how can I love myself or others without knowing that I need and want the love of others? Yet, my world surrounds me with the message that this yearning at my heart's core is *selfish*, and so if I dare to look at it, I must endure guilt and shame—at least momentarily. Guilt because my world has told me that I do not deserve to be loved and given to, that I haven't the right to want it; and shame because I have believed this lie. Despair comes when I face my yearning fully and mistakenly believe that no one could ever fulfill it, so vast, so cosmic is its depth within me. Truly, no single human being could fulfill it, but the Holy One who made me can fulfill it, yearns in turn toward me to fulfill my deepest longings for love, for gifts of love. The Holy One, my Creator, waits to give me this fullness, waits for my readiness to receive. And the fullness comes through others—the composite of all who love me throughout my life—as well as directly through my depths. Many others—friends, lovers, strangers, all creatures great and small become the messengers and bearers of this love for me from my God. When I clear out the shrine at my center, inviting out anyone whom I have erroneously allowed to take the place of God in my life, then the Holy One is free to come and fill me to overflowing. No human being can bear for long the burden of being an idol in my God-center, and the idolatry cripples me and keeps me prisoner to a false religion where no one is allowed to receive and giving is a sham. The other cannot bear the unrealistic expectation and I cannot bear the frustrating disappointment. But I need not despair. I need not pretend that this meager loving is enough.

Clear, now, about my source, I can face those hidden parts of myself, and know that I am more than lover and giver! I can dare to say I Want More!

Loving isn't enough. I want to be someone's miracle! I want to be someone's beloved, someone's most precious gift. *I want to be loved.*

Not wanting to be loved and wanting to be loved fight within me. The not-wanting is only a false form of self-protection from the disappointing thought that I can never be loved enough. Being loved totally, and loving totally—that is the dream of which I despair. But it is more than a dream. It is a life-necessity to me. Not to face it is to yield to fear, and to be condemned to the cold that is the evil on earth. Not to own that I want to be loved is the same as choosing for myself the opposite of love and completion: indifference and isolation. So I admit it. And I accept the frustration of it. And I open myself to the new possibility of it.

Why can't I be loved enough? My need and desire are no greater than anyone else's. Can we then love one another enough? Can we be bearers of our Creator's gifts? Only if we all take on the responsibilities of love. It isn't enough to be protectors and providers; it isn't enough to serve and to give. These can all be substitutes for the real expansion of being that love requires.

Love begins when desire and delight meet. As delight can be destroyed by disgust—the failure of love to sustain and enhance two beings together— desire can be destroyed by distrust, disbelief, distance, dishonesty, denial, deprivation, and despair. Love can be undermined by deception. To be true to love, we need to stop deceiving ourselves about our capacity to love and be loved, about our limits for love; we need to conceive ourselves anew in order to be free to receive from one another. This is the beginnning of being, in love: to end the deceiving in order to begin conceiving ourselves anew, and then to receive love really, commiting ourselves to the elimination of the enemies of delight and desire. Together we undo those tangled wires and replace them with the woven, reuniting threads of trust, belief, closeness, honesty, acceptance, fulfillment. These untie us from our old bonds and reunite us with the health within us, the healing between us.

Becoming a new being and living in love is not to be self-centered, but to be a self, centered in the moving wheel of love as it spins your life in many directions. To become at home in yourself and in the beloved, to find your place in time and space, in your own bodily being, in your spiritual reality, in the cosmos and in eternity.

I can only become ready for this myself by claiming the whole of my search for love, and joining you on the journey. This means facing the pain of not being received by others, and facing my own reasons, gains, and losses for not receiving others. This means acknowledging my own stinginess toward myself and others in giving inadequately of myself, and also seeing the disastrous effects of giving too much. Loving and giving are not synonymous. It is unloving to feed a child more than she wants or needs. Saying "Eat, Baby, eat because I love you and am giving you this food," and then forcing it down her throat will only make her choke or get sick—a cruel way indeed to show love. Whether an imbalance in giving or receiving—both defeat love.

My fear of my own need to be loved is connected with my fear of my own power. I think everyone has the secret terror that "If others really knew me as I am, it would be too much. They would run from me." We have exaggerated notions of our own power. Often this results in our stifling of ourselves. Afraid we'll say too much, we say nothing. Afraid we'll do too much, we do nothing. Afraid we'll give too much, we give nothing. We become what we say, do, and give—nothing. More than anything, I am afraid that I will overwhelm you with my need for you, so I deny it, hide it from both of us. To me, it has the frightening power of an uncontrolled tidal wave. Both of us seem very small in its wake, two small seagulls, too young to know how to ride such waves without drowning and being destroyed in them. I am under the illusion that I protect us both by preserving the lie of my self-containment. I am not self-contained or self-sustained. I overflow myself all the time. But I do not want you or anyone else to know this. My danger will drive you away. No. This, too, is illusion.

The truth is not so dramatic. Other things may drive you away, true, but I am not a mighty ocean wave, most of the time. Most of the time, I am merely an ordinary, commonly eccentric, self-doubting human being, given to expressing my need for love in obtrusive and tricky ways:

> I have a face
> that artists love—
> perfect asymmetry
>
> prefer Kahlua
> for breakfast
> cross
>
> my sevens
> affectedly
> and paint
>
> in scarlet
> impasto.
> Do you want me in your life?

I've spoken about the things that defeat love and conflict with love's intentions to enhance, expand, and complete a being according to that being's nature. There are also conflicts within love itself. The need to give love can conflict with the need to receive love. How many times as a woman I have allowed my own being to diminish in order to give love to others! Now I know that love itself was diminished, because love is only fulfilled in the complete meeting between two complete individuals, and if one of the individuals is made incomplete, the meeting itself is false. As a woman I am now learning at last that I do not have to forfeit my life in order to have relationships with others, especially with men, for whom I have so often mistakenly renounced my life. Wanting the love of others secretly but intensely, my insidious need became self-defeating and destructive when I gave up my own qualities in order to please—and only succeeded in making myself unlovable. Having given up my self-respect, I had no means of attracting respect from others, and being placed last in their value system, I came to value myself less and less, seeing my image shrinking and receding in their eyes. The place of redemption is where Agape and Eros meet again.

When I first looked at my own image, I saw that love was a necessity to me, and I sought ways of calling upon love within my life. I saw the two faces of love, Agape and Eros, radiating within the faces of those who loved me, and reflected within my own loving being as I reached out toward others, and as I learned to love myself. The silver and gold faces of love shine differently as aspects within me and within others.

I could see myself as lover, in the presence of Agape wishing others well and acting for their well being, and in the presence of Eros desiring to be in relationship with others, to create new forms, new shapes of being with them. And I saw myself receiving these same gifts from others who extended these faces of love toward me. What I did not see in either my loved ones or myself was the other side of love, the hidden and contained side we keep closed up deep within ourselves.

The other side of love is the side of the beloved. I showed my open, lover's countenance to myself, but I kept secret the unreasonable features of the one within me who would be loved. She is the beloved who can never believe that she is really loved. She is the part of me that never sleeps, that lies waking, consuming herself with endless longings to be loved, to be held, to be cherished, to be worshipped. She holds her own counsel, afraid that if she speaks I'll call her "selfish" and subdue her. And I have been cruel to her in the past. I failed to hear her, failed to show her mercy and patience, failed to reassure her. I have failed myself most deeply.

Now I face you, beloved being, child of the universe, woman of God, holy creature so long neglected. I hear your cry of desperation. You do not know yet how to unite love's longing toward yourself with love's longing toward others, but you will learn this deepest communion of all—without shame, without guilt, without despair.

I free you, now, to claim the gift of Agape toward yourself: long for your being well. Wish yourself well. It is good for you to desire your own health and holiness of being. You have only to bring this hidden aspect into the open aspect of Agape you feel for others. When there is conflict between your well being and the well being of another whom you also love, you may have to choose. The choice between the wholeness of yourself and the wholeness of another is rarely required, and is the most agonizing of all choices. When it confronts you, ask God's guidance and be faithful to yourself. You can let the beloved other go, entrusting that person's wholeness to God, but you cannot let yourself go. If you choose to sacrifice some part of your life for a beloved other, you must find a way of redeeming the loss of yourself in some new resurrection of your own being, or your sacrifice will not be redemptive for anyone. Between ultimate self-preservation and ultimate self-sacrifice there is the possibility for redemptive love. This love acts for the good of the whole. I cannot tell you anything more about it because I do not yet know anything more than I have told you. Do not tear yourself apart should such a choice be required of you, but make it prayerfully, gracefully, faithfully, and quickly.

On the whole, you are going to remain free to express desire for your own well being and that of others, and this freedom will free others to do likewise. Your relationships with others will become more wholesome as they become more mutual in the quest for wholeness. The wholeness and well being of the relationship depend entirely on the wholeness and well being of the partners.

I free you also to experience the gift of Eros toward yourself fully. As you long to love others with your whole being, you also long to be loved in your whole being. Your desire to be loved is infinite, your longing to be received and given unto is without limit. As you acknowledge this truth within you, you will cease to turn others away by the insidious, sideways seeping of petty demands and clinging possessiveness that so destructively replace the forthright admission of this great desire of yours simply to be loved. As you enter into loving communion with all the parts of yourself and experience the mystical marriage within yourself, all your many selves getting together, their broken pieces healed in a marriage of peace, you will cease to repel others with the impossible plea, "Love me, make me complete." As you love yourself into completion, communion, and internal union, you will become more lovable. The love you sought so frantically and with such inevitable frustration from others will come to you without effort, without struggle. Being loving, you will attract love. Your desire toward others will merge with your full-filling desire toward oneness within yourself. Showing yourself worthy of love and capable of communion by loving and communing within your own person, others who are also worthy and capable will be drawn to you.

Here the conflict between Eros toward yourself and Eros toward others will be less heart-rending, more clear. If being in relationship with another means that you can no longer relate to yourself or your soul's necessary work, and that you are no longer at-one within yourself and with life, then you must forsake the other. For your own sake and the sake of the work God has called you to do and the life you are given to live, you must choose to create relationships only with those who can be mutually nurturing, so that together you may enhance the inner communion between God and creation. In time, your desire for relationship will conform more and more with your desire for internal union and communion. Fragmenting and one-sided relationships will gradually become impossible for you.

Open your eyes to your freedom and great power to love, and the contradictions will harmonize into a single binary truth: nothing is perfect and everything is perfect!

I speak to all of you at once now, to the hidden facets of the prism that is my Self, beginning to shine forth and show yourselves as integral aspects of a single crystalline being. I speak to the human beings, women and men, whom I love and who live inside me because I love you. I speak to the children, born and unborn, who nurture and inspire me. Take courage: love bravely, live boldly. There are limits of time and flesh, yes, but within these, great love can emerge and bless you with bliss beyond words.

I promise you that even though love has taught me that

> holding you close
> with open arms
> it is impossible
> to love sufficiently . . .

yet, I understand
> right here in the paradise
> of your neck, heaven exists
> so that human beings can
> finally be loved enough.

And *"heaven is within you."*

My God-center is open. Here, to this loving place of light and depth within me, I invite the Holy Spirit of Love to come and reside. Here the Holy One will find welcome, and a home. No idol lives here, here no dying lesser god hides, but the One-Who-Is alive in all things lovingly forever resides. I am not alone. I carry all ways the Origin within, and I am eternally pregnant with the Creator of Life, Who is my most intimate companion, Who sings to me from within my own marrow. I am filled with Original Grace.

And this God-pregnancy makes me large enough to meet all life lovingly.

The Loving Composite of God alive within me and every single being I meet is the key to infinite longing's fulfillment. What no idol can achieve through any effort is effortlessly given by the sum of the prismatic Love of God, touching me tenderly and firmly in all creation: through every loving being I've encountered in my whole life.

The all-fulfilling and Loving One is the creative composite of every smile I have sent forth and received, of every kindness shared, of the miracle of every woman, man, and child alive in all times; of every affectionate, lovely, strong, intelligent animal whose beauty and miraculous power I have seen and felt; of every tree that's filled my eye with pleasure or given me shelter; of every raindrop that has calmed, refreshed, or driven me inward to rest and wonder; of every flower that's shared its beauty with me; every modest rock, shifting river, powerful waterfall, or graceful rose; every desert that's revealed new lights and subtle harmonies of color: every thing on earth and within Cosmos is a finger of God touching me with love and delighting in my loving response. And yes, I am loved enough. I am fully filled, truly to overflowing. I can hold nothing back now. I must respond with eager praise in a life that can only be a song of gratitude, a promise of gift, in answer to the Spirit of Love in Creation:

> This is my body
> born for you

> This is my blood
> wherein we make
> life out of me

> are reborn together
> in the new selves
> of our final age
> before the long slow
> opening into eternity

> without despair
> without restraint
> without limitation
> without end

Transfiguration

Shudder of wings.
It happens.
The body becomes
translucent.
A sudden illumination
of bone, all eye—

We see what we love
as never before,
all the way through
in compelling compassion.

Radiant love
pours forth
in true beauty
of being,
fulfilling
the time.

Shudder of wings.
It's over.
Complete in the moment.

The light gives itself
and cannot be denied.

It cannot be summoned.
It cannot be held.
It belongs to itself.
It will happen again,

coming in glory,
again and again,
beyond memory
and before time,

each time
as never
before.

Home delivery
from
Sheed & Ward

Here's your opportunity to have bestsellers delivered right to you. Our free catalog is filled with the newest titles on spirituality, church in the modern world, women in religion, ministry, small group resources, adult education/scripture, medical ethics videos and Sheed & Ward classics.

Please send me a free Sheed & Ward catalog for home delivery.

NAME _____

ADDRESS _____

CITY _____ STATE/ZIP _____

If you have friends who would like to order books at home, we'll send them a catalog to —

NAME _____

ADDRESS _____

CITY _____ STATE/ZIP _____

NAME _____

ADDRESS _____

CITY _____ STATE/ZIP _____